Gardenscapes

DESIGNS FOR OUTDOOR LIVING

Gardenscapes
DESIGNS FOR OUTDOOR LIVING

FOREWORD BY
Martha
Stewart

Carol Soucek King
M.F.A., Ph.D.

PBC INTERNATIONAL, INC.

Distributor to the book trade in the United States and Canada
Rizzoli International Publications Inc.
through St. Martin's Press
175 Fifth Avenue
New York, NY 10010

Distributor to the art trade in the United States and Canada
PBC International, Inc.
One School Street
Glen Cove, NY 11542

Distributor throughout the rest of the world
Hearst Books International
1350 Avenue of the Americas
New York, NY 10019

Library of Congress Cataloging-in-Publication Data
King, Carol Soucek.
Gardenscapes : designs for outdoor living / by Carol Soucek King.
        p. cm.
    Includes index.
    ISBN 0-86636-435-8 (alk. paper). — ISBN 0-86636-410-2 (pbk. alk. paper)
    1. Gardens—Design. 2. Landscape architecture.
    3. Gardens--Pictorial works. 4. Landscape architecture—Pictorial works. I. Title.
SB473.K564 1997   97-3548
712'.6—dc21   CIP

CAVEAT—Information in this text is believed accurate, and will pose no
problem for the student or casual reader. However, the author was often
constrained by information contained in signed release forms, information
that could have been in error or not included at all. Any misinformation
(or lack of information) is the result of failure in these attestations. The
author has done whatever is possible to insure accuracy.

Color separation by AD.VER.srl, Bergamo, Italy
Printing and binding by South China Printing Co. (1988) Ltd., H.K.

10 9 8 7 6 5 4 3 2 1

Printed in Hong Kong

To those who aspire to a lifetime in the garden —

May it surround you with beauty and joy.

May it teach you its songs.

To the garden —

May you surround us with your beauty, your joy and your
universal language of earth, sun, water and seed.

May you teach us your songs!

Contents

Foreword

Those of us who love our gardens are constantly searching for more ideas as we shape them into their most beautiful expression of our envisioned ideal. Perhaps the first rule when planning a garden, or enhancing an existing one, is to take the time to research and discover other gardens through reading and traveling.

By presenting gardens that are creative and accessible, Carol Soucek King has provided us with an abundance of stimulating new ideas. *Gardenscapes* is a wonderful resource for those of us who view gardening as an art form and our gardens as "works in progress." I am always delighted to add a new book to my shelves on a subject that has given me years of boundless pleasure.

Martha Stewart

Introduction

Welcome to *Gardenscapes: Designs for Outdoor Living* — thirty-five residential gardens planned, planted, detailed and sculpted for the individual lifestyles of the people who live in them.

Reflecting the aspirations and passions of their owners and responding to their emotional as well as physical needs, these gardens truly are designed for living — the concept which inspired this volume for PBC International. We did not want just another garden book or a botanical survey, but a book that would be about how people live in their gardens. For that is a garden's true purpose, is it not? How you play there, entertain there, relax there, work there. How it affects your body, your mind, your spirit, your soul.

The expertise required to create a garden that meets all needs, of course, is enormous. To create a garden responsive to a region's microclimate ... and its macroclimate. To enable a garden to be enchanting even while it's new ... and also to have an aesthetic distinction that will endure not only throughout the seasons, but after years of maturation. To integrate a garden into its own unique situation of orientation to the sun, view, access, slopes, drainage and privacy, not to mention its orientation to architecture, to place.

However, expertise is only part of the story. As we visit the following gardens, join us not just in sharing some of their creators' expertise, but also in the feeling they successfully impart. Feel, in some, the Zen-like calm meant for meditation ... in others, the exotic and festive sensuality meant for entertainment. Sense the scale, the proportion, the texture ... and the fragrance!

Whether formal or rustic, expansive or intimate ... whether used for growing herbs, vegetables and flowers or simply playing croquet, every outdoor space in *Gardenscapes* is designed to integrate nature into people's everyday lives in ways that are enriching, highly experiential and deeply meaningful. So, above all, enjoy!

Carol Soucek King, M.F.A., Ph.D.

Eastern Inspirations

astern Inspirations Eastern

Zen-Like Simplicity

Christopher Cox never planned this courtyard garden in Southern California to have such a strong Japanesque influence. It just grew from the language of the site and the clients' needs.

"Added to the simplicity of Buff, Smith & Hensman's architecture was the fact that the clients' forecourt was flat and did not need to serve any purpose save ingress and egress," says Cox. "In addition, when the clients reviewed ground covers, they said they wished there might be something lower than anything I could show them. So I thought, 'Why not gravel?'"

A Zen garden, based on the idea that raked gravel should symbolize the ocean's tides, creating patterns around rocks, or islands, seemed the ideal answer. In addition, the gravel would never have to be watered and, since the clients have no children living at home, would need only infrequent raking. Furthermore, a Zen garden, like this site, must be perfectly flat. And finally, the architects' ceremonial entry that bridges a reflecting pool would lend itself well to a koi pond. The contemporized version of a Zen garden that Cox drew is in complete harmony with the home's minimalist serenity. The highly edited variety of plantings corresponds with the home's limited materials palette. The garden's black granite border serves as preamble to the interior flooring. The garden's blooms, all white except for two pink tabebuia trees and one lilac wisteria vine, echo the architecture's limited color palette. Even the pool's tile — so precisely designed and executed that there is not one cut piece — projects a sense of Zen-like calm.

The entry gate opens to a view across bridge and koi pond to the rear of the garden and its focal point — a vertically placed boulder and coral tree [above]. *The garden, divided by concrete aggregate, tile and koi pond into quadrants, has been raked in four directions, culminating in symbolic tidal movement around the boulders* [opposite].

Photography by Anthony Peres

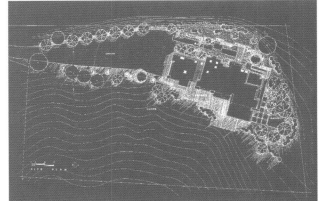

Landscape gardener Howard Oshiyama brought 25 tons of native granite boulders to the site from which Christopher Cox selected and placed the ones he deemed best — devoid of chipped edges and with strong white and black markings [left].

Minimally Sculpted

The simplicity of the garden at Elangeni (Zulu for "Place in the Sun") was inspired by the owners' interest in minimal sculpture as well as landscape designer Diane Sjoholm's personal reaction to the understated character of the house.

For this residence located in Bridgehampton, New York, and used by a husband and wife as their summer home, Sjoholm utilized oriental elements, such as a solid granite bridge and the riverbed of plant materials it spans, as tools to define areas without closing them off visually. "We needed to maintain expansive lawn and garden views throughout the property while creating separate areas for sculpture, privacy, outdoor dining and points of interest," she explains.

A welcoming trio of miscanthus grass, Russian olives and black pines can be viewed most dramatically across the lawn from the property's entrance. Other plantings, such as a simple evergreen backdrop of large junipers, look as if they somehow had always been there, offering a surprise element as one rounds a bend while walking in the garden. These and other garden areas have been designed within the garden to accommodate sculptures by Joseph McDonald and Robert Holmes.

Along with the olives and pines, privet and native cedars have been incorporated, as all four species are strong enough to withstand the site's intense environment. In addition, the miscanthus grass, tolerant of the strong winds and the high water table, looks glorious blowing in the breeze.

A riverbed of plant materials separates and defines garden areas while the granite bridge invites strolling from one to another [above]. *The "river" is planted with juniper and dusty miller to create the feeling of water, over which a Japanese lantern floats on a "raft" of cantilevered bluestone* [opposite].

Photography by Elizabeth Glasgow

Beyond the entry, an interruption in the berm, retained by vertical bluestone and framed with massed plantings of perennials and grasses, leads past another Japanese lantern to the cutting garden [opposite]. The solid granite bridge and spheres create a transition from the open garden area into the more private space under the arbor, its intimacy emphasized by massed plantings [this page].

The arbor is planted with climbing roses and protectively bordered by massed plantings that are composed of grasses and perennials in the dry river garden [right]. *Vertical bluestone defines and protects the cutting garden, where massed plantings of perennials, annuals and herbs provide cut flowers as well as another garden experience* [below]. *A symmetrical layout, wide paths of lawn and inviting benches promote comfortable tours through the cutting garden* [opposite].

Randal Fujimoto, *Landscape Architect*
Honolulu, Hawaii

Indoor/Outdoor Serenity

The traditional *kamaaina* style of this home in Honolulu called for a garden that also would emphasize the informal, gracious style of Hawaiian living. The architecture, constructed of fine-stained redwood with natural stone floors, made use of, rather than fought, the natural elements of sun and breeze. It was landscape architect Randal Fujimoto's pleasure to integrate it with the outdoors.

"Giving special meaning to this project was the fact that it was for an older, well-traveled woman who had long been interested in Southeast Asian art," says Fujimoto. "However, at this particular time of her life, her husband required 24-hour nursing assistance and making the garden entrancing would add a meaningful dimension to his homebound condition."

Through the use of numerous garden elements of hardscape and softscape leading right up to the shoji-like sliding doors, Fujimoto made the garden visually accessible from every room and filled with sensory stimulation. Water and waterplay proved vital to his concept, as did plants of varying texture, color and fragrance. Works of art in the garden add further highlights. To solve the challenge of the site's flatness, he raised certain areas through mounding, massing plants and designing a redwood deck. To tie together formerly segregated areas, he repeated design elements such as river stones, boulders and brick pavers.

Most important, the harmonious blend of all this garden's various aspects with the house itself enriched the client's husband's later years — and made her favorite work of art not one item at all, but the entire environment.

A sculpture garden accents the interior with the fine textures of Lignumvitae, nandina, natal plum and iris set in a bed of river stones [above]. *The repetition of design elements — mondo and zoysia grasses, jaboticaba, guava, iris, hawthorn and allspice — leads the eye through this garden canvas* [opposite].

Photography by **Augie Salbosa**

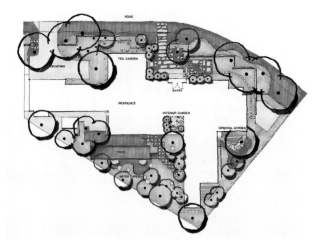

The view from the bedroom offers the sound, sight and cooling effect of water without going outside [opposite]. The redwood deck has been stained a light gray to make sure nothing disrupts the garden's serenity, such as that proffered by a ballast stone sculpture surrounded by mock orange, hawthorn, mondo grass and Surinam cherry [left].

Kinsaku Nakane and Shiro Nakane, *Landscape Architects*
Fukuoka City, Japan

Traditionally Symbolic

Designed for a married couple and their daughter, this garden in Fukuoka City reflects the Japanese tradition of *karesansui*, a dry landscape in which a water-imbued landscape is symbolized. In this case, the feeling was accomplished through white granite gravel, Shirakawa-zuna, or sand from the Shirakawa district.

Created by the late Kinsaku Nakane and his son Shiro Nakane, the garden represents magnificently grand seascapes. This dry landscape is similar to an Indian ink painting (*suiboku-ga*) on a three-dimensional canvas, only here the canvas is the sandy gravel. It is supplemented by trees, including Japanese yew, Japanese and Korean pines, Japanese cedar, tea scent, Ubame oak, ring-cupped oak, magnolias, Japanese pittosporum and Japanese maple.

Bushes — azaleas, Rose of Sharon, camellias, gardenias, winter daphne, apricots and box-leaved holly — are also part of the definitive palette. All are arranged around "seaside vistas" composed of three local rocks, Minou, Mannari and Shiiba, with every vignette paying tribute to water as the source of life.

The most unusual aspect of this otherwise highly traditional garden, primarily used for viewing and walking, is that the main panoramic view is offered immediately — as soon as guests enter the home's entry. Otherwise, it is business as usual — a perfect offering to peace of mind!

The approach to the entry gate beneath an arching Japanese red pine is paved with granite and bordered on one side by a traditional Japanese roofed wall, by a green belt of Macranthum azaleas on the other [above]. *A stone bridge at the garden's entry begins the series of symbolic landscapes* [opposite, above left]. *A stone tsukubai (water basin), a stone lantern and an old camellia provide a hospitable welcome* [opposite, above right]. *Mochi trees, Japanese yew, Japanese red pine, Japanese black pine, Japanese zelkova and Japanese cedar represent the woodlands that might have grown along the banks of a great river* [opposite below].

Photography by Shiro Nakane

Stones symbolize a waterfall cascading down the face of a steep mountain and flowing under the stone bridge, represented by a thin, flat slab of Ryokudei-hengan (green mud metamorphic rock), to the great river, represented by Shirakawa-zuna sand [opposite page]. *The view from the main window at the entry hall reveals a striking panorama of stone bridges, azaleas, Japanese maples, black pines and red pines representing a natural mountain landscape* [below].

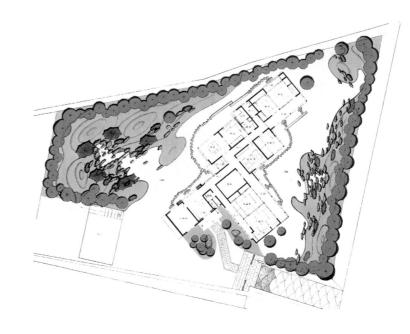

Exotically Eclectic

Timeless, yet with an exotic oriental flair — these were the qualities designer Mark Zeff wanted to impart to the room, walkway and garden he was assigned for the Rogers Memorial Library Showhouse on Long Island, New York.

The room was extremely narrow and long, and the garden area was an odd, triangular shape. "But along with such peculiar dimensions came freedom," he says. "It was as if they demanded an equally unusual, artistic response."

Zeff's answer was to create a haven for some imagined traveler with exotic tastes, and he searched memories of his own travels for inspiration. For the open triangular space, he created flags from natural cotton prints, an interpretation of wedding flags he had seen in a ceremony in Bali, then set them sailing over a tranquil sea of smooth, white stones. At the formerly stark and uninviting wall facing the garden, he installed a three-paneled wooden trellis and accented it with two oriental-style panels. And along the rough-hewn stone walkway leading to the room, he strategically placed a few flashes of color to provide a dramatic sense of arrival — columns painted kelly green; striped awnings of rust, ochre, tan and yellow that turn the doors into caravan tents; and a shrine of dusty green desert grasses.

Says Zeff, "As is often the case, the more difficult the project, the more license one has to be totally different."

A hand-pounded Moroccan brass tray serves as a receptacle for the accent greenery placed outside the caravan-inspired doorway [above]. *The handmade lantern, also from Morocco, adds to the captivating Middle Eastern motif* [opposite].

Photography by Eric Striffler

Kelly-green columns, desert grasses and awnings in desert hues create a Sahara-like atmosphere around the entrance to the room [right]. *An oriental-style panel and a wrought iron plant stand accent the entrance of the traveler's room* [opposite].

Balinese-inspired wedding flags were created of all-natural cotton fabrics from Osborne & Little. The flags' triangular shape was echoed by the lines of the rock garden, subtly emphasizing the contrast between hard, natural stone and soft, pliable textiles [opposite, above and left].

Different geometrical patterns were chosen
for the wedding flags to achieve a sense of
Oriental symmetry and to create interest
through minimal details [above].   The
wooden trellis was made not only to support the kimono-inspired wall hanging,
but also to introduce another natural
material to this courtyard garden [right].

A Mediterranean Look

Dennis Jenkins and Sunny McLean, *Designers*
South Coconut Grove, Florida

Calculated Harmonies

Reality is blurred in the colorful world interior designer Dennis Jenkins and tile merchant Sunny McLean have created, integrating subtropical flora with a fantastic assemblage of stone, tile and glass mosaics in their garden in South Coconut Grove, Florida.

Jenkins and McLean designed both the garden and the house to be viewed as art. For example, they suggest that vistas and sub-vistas be read like a cinematic sequence of events, and that their purposeful layering of visual points of interest be read like a painting as they are viewed from different perspectives.

Scale, texture and color all play important roles here, creating calculated harmonies both visceral and sublime. There is a purposefully false sense of proportion: Because of the fecundity of the foliage, certain vignettes, though in fact quite small, appear grandly voluminous. There is a total envelope of a lush sensuality with one's only possible escape being through the framed vista overhead of the extraordinary Florida sky. There is a kaleidoscope of hues, with floral brilliance playing off the red, purple and gold-painted limestone walls and terracotta tile roof in constantly changing patterns. The ground plane, as well, is broken by alternating areas of cantera stone and concrete pavers, serendipitously placed.

Every aspect seems romantically free, natural and random — but in fact is part of an intellectual exercise in which views are predetermined and vectors are purposefully mismatched or accented. All speak to the importance of letting art infuse every aspect of life and allowing artful fantasies to become reality.

A Chinese fan palm and a column sheathed with Brazilian tile shards and entwined with red bougainvillea welcome guests to Villa Malaga's tropical warmth [above]. *Chinese fan palms frame a terracotta fountain* [opposite].

Photography by Lanny Provo

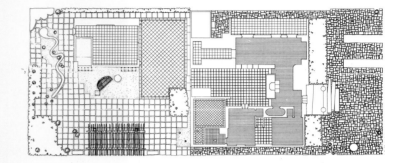

Exclamations of black-and-white checkerboard tiles juxtaposed with Mexican cantera stone are cooled by a collection of subtropical ornamentals and orchids and bordered by an aralia hedge overhung with red bougainvillea [opposite]. *Schefflera and a green thatched palm reach to the sky along with Jenkins's symbolic tower with glass mosaics. Decorative borders include Mexican heather, pentas, Boston ferns and potted* Dracaena marginata [above]. *Treasured specimens include bonsai ficus and tropical ornamentals* [left].

Willow furniture is set in a haven of orange bougainvillea and a trellis covered with copper leaf and staghorn fern [below]. Mozart & the Mysterious Stranger *by Dennis Jenkins is framed by a rebar trellis planted with red, orange and purple bougainvillea* [right].

Red limestone walls provide a rich backdrop
for potted philodendron, spider plants, ant
plants and tropical ornamentals [opposite].
A pepper plant keeps company with rusted
steel wire tables designed by Dennis Jenkins
[above].   A red limestone wall inset with
Florida keystone features potted coleus [right].

Nancy Hammer, *Landscape Designer*
Seattle, Washington

Mediterranean Inspiration

Fine artist as well as landscape designer, Nancy Hammer approaches each garden as a sculptor might, evaluating its impact from each direction and change in level. For this garden overlooking Lake Washington in Seattle, she responded to the site's hot, south-facing exposure and the clients' love of Italian gardens and lifestyle and modeled the property into a series of Mediterranean-inspired, softly hued spaces.

"The design cried out for the sort of drought-tolerant plants that thrive on Mediterranean hillsides," says Hammer. "And, despite the myth that Seattle has an eternally wet climate, this property is so sandy, well drained and sunbaked that water tends to drain away immediately." Using her preference for a palette rich with native materials and ornamental grasses, Hammer created five garden rooms, each with its own distinct character and function. Each unfolds into the next, creating a continuous flow of hardy plantings such as sea kale, strawberry trees and artemisia; Spanish daisies tumble over serpentine, quarried granite walls.

The raised granite terrace at the property's west end overlooks a crushed-stone terrace designed for dining and entertaining. The clients enjoy opening the French doors from the kitchen and bringing good food and music out to where guests are embraced by the sparkling iridescence of drought-hardy fountain grass. A colonnade of upright hornbeam trees creates a lacy privacy screen, while drifts of red switch grass flutter beyond.

"Typically, grasses require little water and tend to mature quickly, filling a garden with abundant color and structure within the first two years," says Hammer.

The rich colors of golden black-eyed Susans and lavender Russian sage play off the bronze New Zealand flax that provides a dynamic architectural form [above]. *Drought-hardy 'Class Act' hybrid tea roses bloom repeatedly throughout the summer. By August, red switch grass and blue asters join in, providing color until frost* [opposite].

Photography by **Steven Young**

Red Japanese maples flutter above heavenly bamboo with a carpet of spotted nettle. Pots with Spanish daisies, spiky dracaena, strawflowers and European balcony geraniums are perched on a granite plinth, providing a strong focal point [left].

Tapestries of contrasting color, texture and scale
are dominant themes as early-season blades of
maiden grass mix with bold yellow black-eyed
Susans and the pale orange of eight-foot-tall sea
kale with ice green, oak-shaped foliage [above].
The entry steps are flanked by cool gray Senecio
greyi, 'Powis Castle' wormwood and rosemary,
with 'skyrocket' junipers, red switch grass, blue
asters and spent Russian sage beyond [opposite].

Ricardo Legorreta, *Architect*
Roger K. Warner, *Garden Designer*
Sonoma, California

Total Integration

To garden designer Roger K. Warner, "A garden does not succeed unless it complements the strength of the architecture while blending with and enhancing the natural setting."

In this case, the architecture to be complemented is that of Ricardo Legorreta, for a home in Sonoma, California. He had been asked to create a weekend retreat for clients who wanted a second home situated in the midst of countryside they adore. "The first task was to choose a location that is spectacular without being imposing," says Legorreta. "The second task was for the massing of the house to be in scale with both the endless landscape and the human requirements of intimacy."

Extending the intimacy of the house into the landscape in a way that would be as natural and simplified yet striking as Legorreta's design, Warner selected 125-year-old 'Sevillano' olive trees with massive gnarled trunks. These grand, mature specimens define spaces and provide shade and sculptural interest, yet they do not mask the geometry of the house that is most dramatic seen against the open blue sky. Forty in all, they are planted in the back and to the side of the house, providing a welcome surprise after the intentionally stark approach.

In addition, many non-native trees and plants were used, but all are compatible with the Mediterranean-like climate. They include 'Owari Satsuma' mandarin orange trees and 'Apricot Sunrise' giant hyssop, the latter attracting hummingbirds throughout the summer and fall.

"The wine country in Sonoma is a place that has soul," says architect Ricardo Legorreta. *"Its rolling hills, the light and deep sense of amplitude and intimacy called for an architecture and garden that fit the context"* [above]. *A field of two thousand lavender plants produces a geometric pattern that reveals the pitch of rolling slopes below the house* [right].

Photography by Lourdes Legorreta

'Sevillano' olives and 'Owari Satsuma' mandarin orange trees, and 'Apricot Sunrise' giant hyssop integrate the architecture into the landcape without concealing its powerful massiveness [above]. *Life takes place around an open courtyard bordering one of Legorreta's trademark celebrations of water as aqua-colored planes in space* [opposite above]. *Deer grass, rosemary, thyme, rockroses and herbs are planted as a wild tapestry to embellish the foreground around the bedroom terraces as one looks to the distant hills* [opposite below].

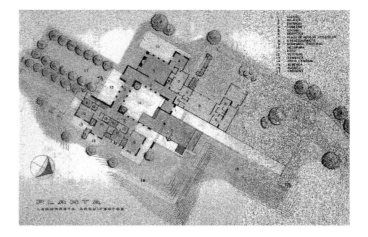

Mediterranean Revival

To the parade of pioneering Americans coming west to escape harsh winters, Californian homes, with abundant gardens warmed by year-round sun and cooled by brightly tiled fountains, have long symbolized total bliss. So it was when this 1920s Mediterranean-revival house in Pasadena was built, but by the time its current owners, both avid gardeners and collectors, moved in, that exterior paradise no longer existed.

Landscape architect Owen Peters of EPT Landscape Architecture took responsibility for its complete restoration as well as the creation of new fountains, ponds, pergolas, sunken gardens, porches, outdoor rooms and the installation of art. However, the process soon became a happily shared experience.

The clients' passion for collecting led them to join in the hunt for the colorful antique tiles that now embellish fountains, walls and tables. And their devotion to gardening soon found them researching what was to become the interesting mixture of flowering trees and plants that would garnish Peters's plan for variously sized outdoor rooms, trellised alcoves, cutting gardens, vegetable gardens, and settings for contemplation. North elevations feature shade-loving ferns and camellias. South-facing gardens are filled with sun-loving roses, succulents, cactuses, aloes, bougainvillea, pittosporum, abutilon, wisteria and pomegranate trees. Ponds are punctuated with papyrus, and, amid towering native oaks and sycamores, palms and tree ferns add tropical notes.

"The result is a garden that is truly a place of discovery," says Peters. "The highly diverse areas unfold like treasures, and, as they bring beauty and joy to the people who live here, they are."

A path of smooth granite cobbles, found in local arroyos and canyons, leads to the garden gate framed by a tile border and overhanging pomegranate tree [above]. *Exotic textures and patterns, including those of the architectural organpipe cactus flanking an ascent to the house from the garden, frame walls and steps* [opposite].

Photography by Steven A. Gunther

The formal core of the garden consists of a
simple rectangular pool adorned with Dutch
delft tiles. Potted roses, king palms, Chinese
flame trees and various other succulents round
out the eclectic planting mix [above].   White
bougainvillea envelops the sturdy pergola,
furnished with seasonal selections from the
owner's orchid collection [left].

Maltese Fantasy

The magic worked in this garden, designed by landscape architect/civil engineer Edward Micallef for his own family in Malta, is that, while its Mediterranean poolside comfort would represent to most people the zenith in outdoor luxury, nothing is overdone. All is in scale with the structure of the house and the people who live there.

Situated on the sunny side of a valley with views toward the bay, the garden consists of a series of Mediterranean-style terraces extending from the residence and evoking a sense of informality that would put anyone at ease. It serves as a sun-drenched extension of the interior, a constantly welcoming beacon to venture outside. The home's light-filled, classically Mediterranean feeling, underscored with white marble floors, spreads outward from every door and window with a mixture of Maltese limestone, white ceramic tile, terracotta tiles and antique stone urns and artifacts. And lining every balcony and patio are glorious celebrations of color and greenery — mostly hardy Mediterranean species such as oleander, date palms, hibiscus, roses, succulents and citrus.

The steep, terraced terrain proved especially well suited to Micallef's planning for the different open-air functions required by his family, which includes three children ranging in age from a 22-year-old daughter to a 5-year-old son. There is a terrace for tea, a barbecue area, a sundeck around the swimming pool for play and relaxation, and an orchard. All are interrelated with passages and terraces and, from all, views of surrounding gardens and the valley below break down the rigidity of formal boundaries and create the illusion of a larger space.

The main entrance porch is flanked by the terraced front garden abundant with rose bushes, hibiscus and an Araucaria *tree, with honeysuckle, blue bellflowers, bougainvillea, and* Stephanotis flori-bunda *as climbers, and a mixture of pink and magenta geraniums and ice plants cascading over the low rubble walls* [above]. *The* Araucaria *tree rises high above the rose bushes, succulents and geraniums, providing a focal point at one end of the front garden which is reached by the curved stone steps* [right].

Photography by Edward Micallef

The short, stone path by the garage is bordered on one side with colorful perennials against a background of creeping ivy [right]. *Terracotta steps descend from the bedroom terrace through a profusion of date palms, oleanders and a variety of succulents and yuccas* [opposite above]. *The pool deck offers an informal gathering of yuccas, hibiscus, ficus and Cycas in the foreground; and date palms, cypress, roses and lantana hedges in the middle. The orchard, with orange, grapefruit, lemon and peach trees, lies sheltered at the garden's lowest level, viewed against a backdrop of the valley beyond* [opposite below].

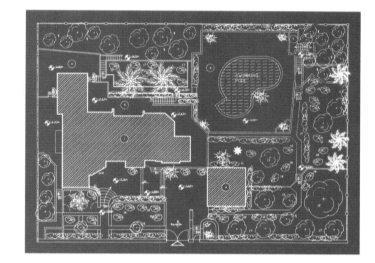

Hugh Dargan and Mary Palmer Dargan, *Landscape Architects*
Atherton, California

Captured Vistas

Ivy-covered slopes, stone-scored stucco columns and custom-designed Italianate gates provide a joyful welcome to this elegant landscape designed by Hugh and Mary Palmer Dargan for a family residence in Atherton, California.

The initial appeal of the site to the new owners was its view of the Palo Alto hills, but its former contemporary landscape was too highly articulated. They wanted a more open plan to accommodate large gatherings as well as their children's play, and a style embracing the sophisticated tone established by the house itself, designed by Norman Askins of Atlanta. Although the footprint of swimming pool, guest house, reflecting pond and tennis court was already established, the Dargans were able to clear enough space for a large, tentable lawn for entertaining and expansive areas for playing ball, croquet and badminton.

In developing the garden aesthetically, the concept of "captured vistas" proved vitally important to the Dargans, and their selection of plants and hardscape evolved totally in conjunction with the major views from the house. For example, the "Jardim de las Vasos" is situated as a backdrop for the dining room. Variegated pieris, rhododendrons and camellias, accented with maidenhair and tree ferns, frame this garden. And in their midst is a family of urns that have been variously designed or selected by the Dargans so their hues of drizzled browns and mossy greens might carry the greens of the interior designed by Jackye Lanham to the outside.

Framed views of other garden rooms reveal an old-fashioned primrose garden, bunny hutch, *azulejos* (a Portuguese tile) spa garden, barbecue garden and reflection pond.

Mop-headed, blue solanum standards add a whimsical note to the flower niche backed with clipped Japanese boxwood hedge inspired by the Filoli Gardens in California. Candytuft, alyssum and dianthus echo the pink color of the tulip magnolias blooming opposite the path [above]. *The rose-bedecked Portuguese gate provides a focal point for the arrival court. The Indiana limestone caps were hand-carved by New Mexico Travertine in Albuquerque, which also supplied the tricolored limestone for the walkways* [opposite].

Photography by Mary Palmer Dargan

Teak benches by Julian Chicester from England provide gracious seating opportunities at entry nodes into the garden and lend a Regency air to the site furnishings [right]. Acorn-embellished terra-cotta jardinieres with tripod bases, custom made at Viuva Lamego in Lisbon, provide pockets of color. Wooden edging holds the crisp lines of the design along garden paths [opposite].

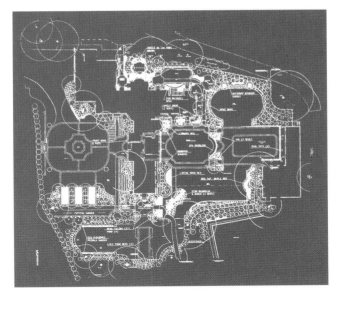

The azulejos (Portuguese tile) spa garden, designed by Dargan Gardens, tells an allegorical story about the family and its travels. Mexican fan palms frame the swimming pool with a tropical air, while blue agapanthus bloom with white potato vine and blue plumbago [right]. The perennial sweep adjacent to the pool provides room for growing citrus in pots, as well as leisurely games of croquet. Seating by Julian Chicester is accented by masses of gray artemisia [below]. The Italian, hand-wrought balustrade, modeled on those found at Sintra near Lisbon, is preceded by blue lobelia, roses and plumbago. Pool furniture, by Florentine Craftsmen, was created especially for this project in a neoclassical design [opposite].

Jardim de las Vasos is a pocket garden modelled after ones seen by the designers at La Frontiera Palace in Lisbon. The custom-carved, five-foot Italian urn from OPI in Los Angeles has a family of smaller urns from Viuva Lamego in Lisbon set against a carpet of blue star laurentia and baby's tears backed with tree ferns. [left and far left]. In the old-fashioned primrose garden, twig-inspired benches painted Charleston green provide a shady retreat from which to watch lawn games [above].

Natural Settings

tural Settings Natural Setti

Neiva Rizzotto, *Landscape Designer*
São Paulo, Brazil

Tropic Modernity

A highly contemporary structure designed by architect Ugo Di Pace hovers over a garden punctuated by hardy succulents and masses of colorful perennials, and enlivened with terracotta vases, statues and sculptures. It is a harmonious dance between the home's structure and its plantscape.

"The garden was created for a family that loves art — the husband is president of Fundacão Bienal in São Paulo," says landscape designer Neiva Rizzotto. "Their collection added to the mixture required to create a modern, tropical image.

Fundamental to Rizzotto's design was selecting plants, trees and shrubs that respond to Brazil's abundant summertime sun — as well as the country's typically plentiful rain and humidity.

She also expressed the aspect for which her garden design is renowned — planning gardens that will flower throughout the year. In spring, this garden is resplendent with orchids, blue plumbago, hydrangea, variously-hued bougainvillea, pink and white azaleas, and red heliconias and rose apple. In summer, it dazzles with white-and-pink impatiens, yellow daylilies and yellow jasmine. In the winter, the garden is honored by white euphorbia, red Heavenly Bamboo, white-and-pink camellias and pink rhododendrons. Bridging the gaps throughout the year with their never-ending glorious blooms are cymbidium orchids; red, white and pink anthuriums; blue daze; yellow chrysanthemums; red copperleaf; alyssum; and orange abutilons.

"Plants were chosen individually and for their beauty in the overall context," says Rizzotto. "The important thing is to not try to be like the rest. Let your imagination go wild!"

Fallen flowers from a eugenia tree create a brilliant carpet leading to the terrace, surrounded also by liquid amber, camellias, begonias, impatiens and spathiphyllum [above]. *Brazilian terracotta vases are set on an uncovered lounge to connect colorful offerings of bougainvilleas, rhododendron, Cocos weddelliano and pruned thuja topiary to the pool, while off-white cotton curtains link exterior and interior* [opposite].

Photography by Ricardo de Vicq de Cumptich and Mauricio Simonetti

The barbecue, of antique Portuguese ceramic tiles and set against Jasminum mesnyi, Euphorbia leucocephala, *eugenia and cypress, serves as gathering place for the family's weekend retreats. Unpolished granite and terracotta squares adorn the pool's surround* [opposite]. *A granite and terracotta stairway leads to the tennis court through an avenue of* Vriesea bituminosa, *bird-of-paradise, Sago palm, ardisia and a Phoenix palm* [above]. *At the swimming pool, a Phoenix palm rises from an encirclement of* Vriesea bituminosa, *evolvulus and begonias.* [left].

Near the swimming pool, a grouping of
allamanda, thuja, evolvulus, begonias,
hydrangeas and palm trees makes a lush
garden [above].   A garden including Vriesea
bituminosa, *anthuriums and a Phoenix
palm, arranged with a Brazilian sculpture
and natural stone, brings the outside into
the dining room* [opposite].

Sherna Stewart, *Landscape Designer*
Carmel, California

Woodland Rusticity

A truly gracious garden reflects the aspirations and inspirations of everyone involved. That is why landscape designer Sherna Stewart says she is so aware that credit for this admirably rustic yet comfortable garden in Carmel, California, must be shared with the architect, the gardeners and her client.

He, a philanthropist/civic benefactor and an outdoorsman devoted especially to cycling and birding, is also a single father with a teenage daughter. His property is located in a native pine and oak woodland above a canyon and reaches down to a canyon greenbelt, accessible to the public, which leads to the historic Carmel Mission San Carlos. It was already pleasant — but he needed more privacy and, on the street side, a garden that would be better suited for year-round entertaining and his preference for informality.

Working with the existing trees and around established forms such as a new garage addition, Stewart enriched and enlivened the redwood shingle home's clean-cut, casual style with more comfortable rusticity. She restored the wooded canyon and, working with the architect, David Smith, added a fence and gate to create privacy, extended the railroad ties to define the garden, and removed part of an existing adobe wall to provide for circulation.

Choosing evergreen grasses and sedge as well as New Zealand flax and filling them out with flowering shrubs and long-blooming perennials, Stewart continued the informality by laying crushed rock in the courtyard and paths leading up to the front door.

Notes Stewart. "Our goal was to retain the natural atmosphere of the woods throughout the garden — only to make it more so."

At the entry, the client's preference for dark, warm, rich colors is carried out with purple pennisetum grass, a wine-colored abutilon, purple heuchera, red dahlias, trailing red geraniums and red trumpet vine. The home's redwood shingle siding was waterwashed, and a fence was added, giving privacy and creating a backdrop for the garden ten feet below it [above and opposite].

Photography by Matthew Onyesco and Kipp Stewart

A courtyard of crushed rock interspersed with railroad ties is shaded
by oak trees and enlivened by lime
and yellow/green variegated foliage
of flax, sedge and helichrysum.
Native columbine and gaillardias
in red and yellow visually connect
the yellows of marigolds and
daylilies with red impatiens.
Honeysuckle at the far corner
sweetens the path to the exercise
room [right]. Windows at the
entry hall and kitchen provide
another view of the entry path,
including the red 'Gartenmeister
Bonstedt' fuchsia [opposite above].
Outside the study, soft and burnt
oranges of lion's tail, monkey
flower, dahlias, hibiscus, 'Apricot
Nectar' rose, Carex flagellifera,
'Cameo' yarrow and pansies soften
an adobe wall [opposite below].

Peter A. Gisolfi, *Architect/Landscape Architect*
Hudson River Valley, New York

A Suburban Villa

It is difficult to believe that a short while ago this home looked like an object in space — seemingly unattached to the land surrounding it and without room for a garden. The house was located so close to a steep, unruly escarpment that only a small patch of grass separated it from the edge and an existing turnaround took up the remaining garden space. Today, however, no trace of that former state remains, for Peter Gisolfi and Iwona Rainer transformed the escarpment as well as the entire property into an entrancing series of indoor and outdoor spaces for living.

Now a terrace, designed in harmony with the home's original seventy-year-old Georgian style, invites rather than prohibits walks to the property's edge. In addition, Gisolfi opened up views of the Hudson River, the Palisades and an old quarry. And in spite of the fact that his clients asked him to design a new entry drive and court, a new four-car garage, a pool house, spa and fitness center, he managed to save all of the property's mature trees. Primarily, however, the driving force behind the transformation of both structure and site has been Gisolfi's personal vision of "the suburban villa," — a series of interconnected indoor and outdoor rooms inspired by the classic Italian villas of the sixteenth century. For this home, Gisolfi's plan provided seemingly endless landscaped connections between the villa's existing spaces as well as both indoor and outdoor rooms for the new pool pavilion. The idea was perfect for the clients, who find deep enjoyment in flowers and trees. Now, to get their fill of myriad grand trees, lush shrubs and, when in bloom, breathtaking decorative plants, they need only walk out any door or look out any window.

Stone pillars and a decorative wrought-iron gate provide a formal entry to the site. The drive leading to the circular turnaround is lined with evergreens, birch, locust, a variety of exotic trees, plus azaleas, climbing hydrangea and blue periwinkle [above]. *A stately oak sits in the center of the romantic garden. Other plantings include mature copper beech trees, dogwood and flowering azaleas with euonymus ground cover* [opposite and overleaf].

Photography by Norman McGrath

Cobblestone curbing circumscribes a small sculpture
garden awaiting art and lines the turf path leading to
spiraling stone stairs built into the fieldstone wall.
Plantings in the foreground include flowering perennials,
periwinkle and ivy [above].   A semicircular retaining wall
in the formal terraced garden overlooks the sculpture
garden, from which informal stone steps lead up to the
romantic garden in the rear [left].

Sense of Enclosure

Interior designer George Constant not only created the interiors for a couple's new residence in Garrison, New York, he instigated architectural changes and then planned the entire landscape, including the pool and gazebo.

"Gardens are a visual extension of an interior," says Constant. "In this garden, as in the house, we wanted the feeling of being enveloped in nature."

In the house, which was prefabricated in Maine and shipped, he made changes right on site to open it up to the setting, ensuring a wealth of natural illumination by adding skylights and open balconies. For the garden and pool, he arranged plantings, rocks and built a trellised structure for a sense of being enclosed within a wooded glen.

The site's existing rocks were Constant's starting point, which he edited and then embellished with Tennessee river stone — large, flat surfaces striated with earthy hues of blue, purple, red and brown. Jutting out into the pool and surrounded by an enormity of pines and evergreens, they make its waters seem to have been there forever, only the house a recent addition.

Between the house and pool is Constant's final but perhaps most prominent ode to being sheltered, but still out-of-doors. Inspired by Japanese garden pavilions, he designed the vine-covered, trellised gazebo with a circle motif, framing the landscape within round openings centered on each side so that a different view is highlighted in each of the four directions.

The gazebo looks outward toward a woodsy setting, its circle motif framing the maples and oaks as if they were works of art. The decorative grasses and bamboo are recent additions [above]. *"In this garden, as in the house, we wanted the feeling of being enveloped in nature." — interior designer George Constant about the cedar structure entwined with fleeceflower* [opposite]

Photography by Peter Vitale

Blue Atlas cedar, dwarf maple and cherry trees as well as the breeze-responsive plume plant join the freely-placed Tennessee river stone to make the new pool seem more like a natural pond [left]. *Old terracotta pots and hanging baskets teeming with impatiens lend softness and color to the shaded dining area. The bench is an antique from England* [below].

Don Monger/The Landmark Group, *Landscape Architect*
Brisbane, Australia

Free Flow

Not far from Brisbane's city center is a garden that seems as completely rural as the outback's furthest reaches. The site, sloping down from a 1980s home catering to light and air in the tropical Queensland style, lent itself to a free-flowing plan, and landscape architect Don Monger fulfilled nature's suggestion with a jungle-like intermeshing of natives, palms and exotic species. *Phoenix roebelenii*, bougainvillea, callistemon, native violets and mondo grass overlap each other in rich profusion while they descend imperceptibly toward the pool.

Totally integrated with the garden, as was the clients' request and as is Monger's specialty, the pool seems at once a completely natural pond and an immensely comfortable habitat for humans. Its black crushed-marble finish, which heightens the reflection of sky and foliage rather than the pool's interior, makes the water's depth as fascinating as some mountain stream discovered on a summer's walk in the woods. Contained by large feature boulders interspersed with railroad ties for decking, its effect is not of anything man-made but of the most natural of grottoes.

Especially addressing Brisbane's sub-tropical climate in species immediately around the pool, Monger selected Alexandria palms, *Melaleuca quinquenervia*, *Bauhinia galpinii* and *Lommandra longifolia*. For family, friends and for their own enjoyment, the clients' dream of an oasis within a stone's throw of the city is a year-round reality.

A gathering of Sydney blue gum eucalyptus, lilly-pilly and tristania trees makes the Queensland-style home seem far removed from its proximity to the city of Brisbane [above]. *The natural-looking pool, freely formed with railroad tie decking, boulders and sculpted logs, seems anything but man-made. Plantings include paperbark, tree fern, Alexandria and dwarf date palms and lommandra grass* [opposite].

Photography by David Knell

Diane Sjoholm/Sirius, *Landscape Designer*
Sag Harbor, New York

Cottage Gone Wild

Design constraints can spur creativity as much as total freedom. So it was with this garden in Sag Harbor, New York, an old whaling village with a National Historic District.

Owned by a woman who uses the home as a weekend retreat for relaxing, gardening and intimate gatherings, this garden had to meet her needs for quiet and privacy. The house itself dates back to the 1850s and, while completely renovated, its centuries-old charm remained and had to be protected. But when landscape designer Diane Sjoholm was greeted with the historical responsibilities in addition to a small narrow site, a deeply descending grade and neighbors just a handshake away, she turned all restrictions into assets.

At the entry, a large chaste tree and flowering shrubs, perennials and annuals respond to the site's historic character. For privacy, Sjoholm created a baffle of yew hedges, which also form an evergreen backdrop for the loosely cottage-style gardens that follow, exploiting the dramatic change in grade from front to rear.

The effect of Sjoholm's making the most of that descending grade is one of "cottage gone wild," for she variously leveled it into a series of highly individual outdoor rooms — a cooking garden abundant with herbs, a green sitting room enhanced with perennials, and, at the rear, a woodland glen verdant with ferns.

On the grassy lower woodland plateau, an aluminum sculpture by architect Ernest Schieferstein, responsible for remodeling the home, echoes the downward spiral of this garden and suggests the idea of spiraling outwards and upwards. It is the ideal culmination for a garden primarily meant for contemplation.

The transition from the sunny perennial garden to a shady area is made more dramatic by oversized, cantilevered New York bluestone slabs [above]. *A wild mass of color and fragrance surrounds the main outdoor deck, creating a cottage feeling. Perennials here include the sunflower-like heliopsis,* Platycodon grandiflorus *and veronica; the annuals are dwarf cosmos, heliotrope, dahlias and calamintha, its mint-like foliage presenting clouds of dainty white flowers from late summer until frost and sometimes longer* [opposite].

Photography by Elizabeth Glasgow

Architect Ernest Schieferstein's
sculpture lends the notion of spiraling upwards to the sun [above].
Masses of hydrangeas, ferns,
hostas, daylilies and other shade-
loving plants create a lush, shaded
environment as the garden spirals
down to its lowest level, a woodland glen [right]. Rock walls create
an intimate spot for sitting along
the path down to the shade
garden. Chairs are painted to
provide a counterpoint to the soft
hues of the plants and stonework
[opposite above]. Long view over the
herb garden into the sun garden,
given privacy by walls of yew
hedges. Tall perennials and
annuals, such as meadow rue,
Joe Pye weed, globe thistle and
dahlias, create an interesting
change of scale [opposite below].

Peter Lindsay Schaudt, *Landscape Architect*
Chicago, Illinois

Urban Tranquility

Escaping from the city in the city — that was landscape architect Peter Schaudt's directive for this garden in the middle of Chicago. Located on four former city lots, it is centered on a piazza as spare as the Modernist-style home it surrounds. Yet, punctuating its starkly flat extensions of Indiana limestone and Merrimac riverstone is a treasure-trove of birch, honey locust, boxwood, serviceberry, viburnum, hydrangea, arborvitae, English ivy, ferns, cotoneaster, fothergilla and winter creeper.

"The riverstone surface was originally selected to accommodate not only the clients' expansive parties but also their two large dogs," says Schaudt. "In the end, however, it also proved integral to the theme of a highly simplified space that would complement the streamlined architecture and the owners' contemporary art."

The carefully selected trees, shrubs and creepers further highlight the works of art and amplify the drama of such a major city garden, with the infusion of a birch grove offering an especially commanding expression of the powerful statement nature can make in an urban context. Serviceberries, a white pine and arborvitaes hover protectively about one cozy corner. A honey locust tree serves as reason to sit and contemplate on a bench by Jenny Holzer. And the birch trees' scale lends a sense of intimacy to Richard Serra's 35-ton, steel octagon; in addition, they offer summer shade and winter interest, their bark blending with the snow.

"The late Max Gordon designed this house to focus out toward the piazza and garden, and Vinci/Hamp Architects helped bring his idea to its successful conclusion," says Schaudt. "I wanted to make sure every view expressed nature's beauty as they intended."

The living room looks out to the piazza, its minimal planting — a birch tree in the foreground and birch grove beyond — continuing the spare sophistication of the home's architecture [above]. View toward the house from the birch grove, with a honey locust on the right [opposite].

Photography by Leslie Schwartz

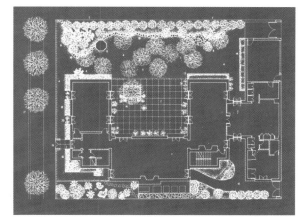

An espaliered pear tree provides a backdrop for the herb garden's lavender, artemisia and perennial lady's mantle [opposite and above]. Merrimac (Wisconsin) river stone, bordered by raised boulders and an arborvitae hedge that screens out the neighboring house, leads to a Richard Serra sculpture, Finkl No.1. The pebbly stone path provides a gentle contrast to the tilted artwork's 35-ton Cor-Ten steel form [left].

On the Water's Edge

Landscape architect Don Monger worked with the owner of this 1950s contemporary Queensland house for several years, not just designing the garden but redesigning the house so that there could be a garden.

Situated on the Nerang River, the narrow site was formerly given over to a predominant driveway and car accommodation. The garage itself was located within the U-shaped house where Monger envisioned a garden should be. By relocating the garage to the front of the property, he could turn that central important area into a recreational room adjacent to the proposed swimming pool — and much, much more.

The revision, which the client immediately accepted, also allowed Monger to commence a water course at an entrance pavilion and let it travel some 70 meters to the swimming pool. A path adjacent to the water course meanders blithely through another pavilion, beside quiet ponds and past cascading waterfalls.

Slate, not a typical material in Australia, was used as paving, and vertical water walls are also of slate in a book-leaf construction. Steppingstones are large slabs of granite. Boulders are weathered sandstone.

The planting took on a tropical style, featuring royal and pigmy date palms, cycads, mondo grass, colorful azaleas and camellias with aquatic plants on the water's edge.

All walls facing this scenic display are outfitted with concertina doors. Not surprisingly, they are always open.

The exotic palm-filled oasis, alive with the sound of gentle waterfalls, is approached by way of wide, slate and granite steps descending by a series of tranquil pools, passing beneath ornate cedar pagodas and terminating at a large stone terrace beside a lagoon swimming pool. The plant selection includes royal and pigmy date palms, cycads, mondo grass, azaleas and camellias [above and opposite].

Photography by David Knell

Stephen F. Mechler, *Landscape Architect*

Oahu, Hawaii

Tropical Tapestry

Designed by Stephen F. Mechler, this Hawaiian landscape provides large open spaces for the clients' family gatherings, outdoor sports activities and occasional landings of their helicopter — all in a setting reminiscent of an English country garden but with a tropical beachside overlay.

"The goal was to take advantage of the magnificent oceanfront view, yet create an intimate series of garden rooms reflecting the clients' love of the islands and their flora and, as does the casual island architecture of their house, the family's prominence in Hawaii's history over the last one hundred years," says Mechler.

An abundance of color, carefully displayed against a tropical backdrop of luxurious leaf textures and brilliant ocean blues, is graced by traditional embellishments. Antique brick paths and motorcourt paving provide a rich, sun-dappled carpet beneath bowers of gardenias and canopies of majestic monkeypod and mango trees. An eighteenth-century whaling pot, formerly used to reduce blubber to oil, has been refitted to become a liquid canvas for an encircling throng of waterlilies. Large whiskey barrels are filled with an ever-changing display of colorful annuals, Swedish ivy and delicate pink tea roses.

Due to the salty and windy oceanfront location, the series of tranquil lanais and garden rooms Mechler created had to be carefully orchestrated to allow many of the sensitive plant materials to survive. For example, fragrant white ginger is planted in the estate's ever-shady and protected "Tropical Alley" section. By protecting its delicate petals, he has provided the clients with a continual supply of blossoms to fashion into Hawaiian floral leis.

Antique brick paving continues from the motorcourt to the intimate entry garden and its lush bower of fragrant tiarella. While not concealing the garden's basically tropical nature, combinations of pastel impatiens, pentas and caladiums, punctuated with masses of blue daze, lavender, otanthus, yellow shrimp plants and silver dusty miller create the casual exuberance of an English country garden [above].

Photography by Gary D. Pietsch/Peach Boys Photo

In a refitted eighteenth-century whaling pot, now given a more sedate use as an oasis for waterlilies, a gently splashing fountain jet creates a subtle acoustical focus for the courtyard [left]. As the property approaches the Pacific, the use of the more delicate exotics is tempered, and the garden opens up to broad grassy expanses framed with towering coconut palms to appropriately host lawn games and sunset viewing [below].

Heavenly Oasis

Halekailani — "house of the heavenly sea" — is located in a hot, volcanic coastal area on the Big Island of Hawaii's Kohala Coast. Situated on the promontory of the Mauna Lani Bay Resort, this dream retreat is subject to high winds, a factor that influenced landscape architect Gregory A. Boyer as he created a lush oasis appropriate for family use.

The traditional Hawaiian-Mediterranean blend found in the architecture of C.W. Dickey can be seen in the structure, and it was to this, both in its scale and feeling, that Boyer responded. Princess and dwarf date palms set the mood in the exterior courtyard, while coconut palms provide appropriate height and sense of place. Silver buttonwood trees complement the gray-green roof tiles. Purple spider lilies, pink dwarf Thai ixora, red bougainvillea and variegated liriope punctuate the house and hardscape's subdued color palette. Large, dramatic geometry trees celebrate the site's majestic quality as well as provide welcome shade.

Yet it was a series of site-specific challenges that inspired some of the garden's most inviting aspects. "It was to lend relief from the desert-like heat that led to the general oasis theme," says Boyer, "while it was the unprotected, flat, oceanfront location that led to our building up layers of plantings to serve as a buffer against the wind. And it was the close proximity to the neighbors that led to the lush density of the plantings that we felt necessary for privacy as well as to define the numerous outdoor sitting areas."

The result represents a commanding yet harmonious marriage of house and garden, a whole that is infinitely better than its parts.

Carpentaria acuminata *palms and a geometry tree provide a graceful arch over the auto court entry, its copper-roofed portico echoing the lines of the home's architecture. Bougainvillea provides color* [above]. *Along the unprotected, flat oceanfront, salt- and wind-tolerant plantings — such as laua'e fern, coconut palms, shrublike wax banyan, and silver buttonwood tree — provide sheilded sitting areas for leisurely whale watching* [opposite].

Photography by Brett Uprichard

Landscape architect Greg Boyer and John Groark, known for his exciting pools and rock formations, worked together to use their complementary skills in creating this tranquil interior courtyard pool garden that can be seen from every area of the house [above].

Lush highlights around the interior pool include colorful splashes of pink crotons, pigmy date palms and a spiky bromeliad. Pool/rockscape designer John Groark's sand finish for the bottom of the pool creates a light green tone — the final touch for this lagoon-like oasis [top and above].

Sidney Galper, *Landscape Architect*
Cleo Baldon, *Designer*
Beverly Hills, California

Playful Adventure

Sidney Galper and Cleo Baldon were the ideal landscape designers for a couple in Beverly Hills who wanted their hillslope yard planned anew for their young daughter's delight. Galper and Baldon had created the garden two decades earlier when the traditional, slate-roofed house had been built. Besides, they themselves delight in garden magic.

The lot is completely surrounded by tall, mature eucalyptus trees left from the large original estate developed early in the century. The new owners wanted to retain this eucalyptus border, of course, but wanted a lawn instead of the existing pool on the flat part of the lot and a new pool that would feel like a mountain lake further down the slope. Commencing a watercourse at the house, the designers let it fall a full story into their newly created rock-rimmed pool. From there, water flows into a stream and over two more falls until it splashes beside the play area at the bottom of the site.

The upper lawn is dominated by two mature coral trees surrounded by a vast palette of flowers and vines that become a lush jungle of green on green as the lot descends. In one place, a fern gully extends from the upper street side to the site's lowest edge. And in the midst of all, cliffs cast from molds of real formations in the high Sierras are proffered for rest or play.

A fescue lawn bordered with bougainvillea now resides where there was once a swimming pool. The new, less conventional pool has taken shape down the slope [above]. *Cascades of bougainvillea bring notes of complementary color to this last waterfall in a water system that begins at the house and descends to the bottom of the property* [opposite].

Photography by Deidra Walpole

Behind the pool's waterfall, softened by rush-like horsetail, a tunnel leads to a rock-lined dressing room and a bar that serves swimmers seated underwater. A fog machine can create a hovering mist over the cascade [right]. The pool, its border punctuated with Japanese iris, is shaped to provide a straight, unobstructed swim in spite of its irregular contours [opposite above]. The brick pillars support the house a level above and define the bar grotto. The waterfall descends from the house and lawn level to the pool and its gathering of Japanese iris and agapanthus [opposite below].

The lot descends in a series of man-made cliffs, impressions of actual cliffs applied to retaining walls and highlighted with Australian tree ferns [right]. An underwater ramp paved in pebbles and flagstone offers a gradual, stepless entry into the pebble-lined pool. It reaches its three-foot depth in about twenty feet, before it can interfere with the swimming lane [below]. At the top of a brick retaining wall, amid an abundance of trailing periwinkle, the water system that descends through natural-looking courses and falls begins here in a spillway more architectural in form [opposite].

Formal Elegance

Emmet L. Wemple, Denis L. Kurutz, Frederick H. Haberecht
Emmet L. Wemple & Associates, *Landscape Architects*
Brentwood, California

Art-Filled Environment

An appropriate environment for the display of art can be as important as the collection itself, for the way art is shown to a great degree determines the way it will be seen.

In 1988, the owners of this hillside home in Brentwood, California, began construction of a gallery space for their art collection. The layout of their property prior to construction consisted of two terraces: the lower occupied by their existing home, and the upper terrace, a tennis court. The late landscape architect Emmet L. Wemple, working with Denis L. Kurutz and Frederick H. Haberecht, used plantings, water, and hardscape to create a parallel sequence of outdoor living and gallery spaces. The new galleries link the front door of the existing home with the sculpture garden on the upper terrace.

Like the architectural spaces, the garden spaces link existing living spaces with new ones, creating subtle environments for the display of art. Central to the design is the visual integration of new garden spaces with the surrounding mountains.

The lower garden and plaza are the primary areas for the display of sculpture and for entertaining, dominated by James Turrell's conceptual work, a 20-foot cube entitled *Second Meeting*. Wemple used exemplary restraint in his landscape here, allowing the art and architecture to frame views. The upper garden is more exuberant in its use of plant materials and more closely aligned with the adjacent mountains in color and texture. The subtle but important contrast between the two areas serves as living testament to a legendary landscape architect's expertise and sensitivity.

Framing a cast-aluminum birdbath by Clarice Dreyer along the nature trail of Bouquet Canyon stone are coral bells, foxglove, montbretia and Korean grass [above]. *At the trailhead above the circular pool, a concrete bench invites visitors to contemplate the surrounding envelope of 'Morning Light' variegated westringia, species geraniums, sweet gum trees and red-hot poker plants* [opposite].

Photography by Jay Venezia

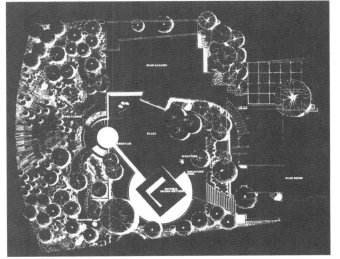

Surrounding James Turrell's conceptual
work and the pool encircling it are massings
of montbretia, foxglove and cape mallow
and a grove of paperbark melaleuca [opposite
above]. A simplified base of Korean grass
sets the silhouette of the gallery wall and
three-part bronze sculpture by Charles Fine
in dramatic relief [opposite below left]. The
circular pool echoes the bowl shape of the
natural terrain above the sculpture plaza,
now clothed with blue hibiscus, California
lilac and star jasmine [opposite below right].
The water elements, within a plane of
Korean grass against a backdrop of tree
ferns, were designed to reflect the sky and
create a linkage between the ground plane
and the James Turrell cube which itself
captures the sky through a circular skylight
within [left].

Structured Simplicity

Understatement marks the landscapes of the SWA Group's John L. Wong — even those with as many demanding criteria as that of this family residence in California.

The children are young and the entire family likes to live, play and entertain outdoors as much as possible. Other considerations included the need to screen neighboring structures on two sides of the triangular property, yet maximize views of a golf fairway and hills on the third side. Finally, the clients specifically requested a variety of water features.

The grounds and residence, developed through close collaboration between Wong and architect Michael C. F. Chan, address all these requirements through a series of circular connections. Circles of external pathways and internal hallways intersect to create a variety of spaces and views, with the circular building defining an internal courtyard for small-scale events and external areas suitable for swimming, lawn games and the children's play garden.

Wong simplified his palette to species that respond well to the California climate and dry, hillside context — coast live oak, California pepper, sweet gum, sycamore, pine, pear and plum trees. Even the hill slopes are hydro-seeded in wildflowers and not irrigated.

As for the clients' request for numerous water features: Wong and Chan provided them with a greenhouse/parlor water stair and lily pond, a reflecting pool encompassing the music room, a water wall and fountain stair in the foyer, and a fountain in the master bedroom. The swimming pool itself is set in a larger garden pool with fountains to enliven the exterior grounds.

A massive oak tree throws its shadows over the main portal from the arrival court, framed by potted geraniums amid perennials and backed by Boston ivy intended to cover the plaster walls in the future [above]. *The paved arc of the interior courtyard leading to the home's front door is framed by sweet gum trees with drifts of flowering azaleas. Ground cover is drought-tolerant fescue grass* [opposite].

Photography by Tom Fox

From the spa, the perennial garden provides an enveloping view of twenty-two beds of English, French and Spanish lavenders as well as daylilies, iris and gardenias that the clients cut for floral arrangements when they are entertaining [right]. *The swimming pool sits in the midst of fountain-enhanced ponds on both sides and is shaded by two Chinese tallow trees against a backdrop of Afghan pine* [opposite above]. *Beside the music room, stepping blocks from the pool terrace lead to a lawn of fescue grass, its circumference defined by a row of sweet gum trees* [opposite below].

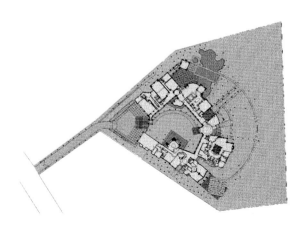

Zuhair H. Fayez, *Architect and Landscape Architect*
Jeddah, Saudi Arabia

Coastal Seclusion

For this family home bordering the Red Sea in Jeddah, Saudi Arabia, privacy, an imperative in the traditional Saudi/Islamic way of life, was as important as opening up the view to the sea. In creating the landscape, Zuhair H. Fayez answered both requirements while infusing the garden's unmistakable grandeur with a sensitivity that creates the feeling of space and proportion demanded by his architecture.

Noted for his entries, each different from the other and each reflecting the individual clients' tastes, Fayez surpassed even his own reputation here at each of the two grand approaches where guests disembark either by automobile or yacht. The nature of the site, which was augmented when Fayez dredged the channel to facilitate the large boats that would be moored there, created the expectancy of a broad, welcoming expanse leading to the power-fully contemporary structure. With palm- and flower-lined tile walkways leading through terraces shaped by river rock walls and covered profusely with multicolored lantana, the garden beckons guests past aloe, yucca, bougainvillea, acalypha, asparagus fern, gardenias and jasmine — but at a leisurely, enjoyable pace. For, throughout the garden, whether at the tiled-roof pavilion at the boardwalk's end, the waterfront gazebo thatched with palm leaves, or the immensely hospitable shaded trellises bordering the pool, there are seemingly endless places to walk, relax and entertain.

By locating service functions such as kitchen and storage on the home's first level, Fayez was able to place the main entry a full story above ground at the top of stairs rising grandly from a carpet of the low, herbaceous Wedelia trilobata *punctuated by graceful royal palms* [above]. *Steps descend to the sea from a dais surrounded by plants selected not only for the color of their flowers, but also for the color and texture of their leaves, such as the light green, waxy leaves of the* Crinum asciaticum *in the foreground* [opposite above]. *A sturdy wooden trellis, developed around the swimming pool and defined by a border of potted fern palms, provides an unrestricted view of the sea from within the house* [opposite below].

Photography by Zuhair Fayez and Associates

Disparate Adventures

A hillside garden of oriental inspiration; vegetable, cutting and formal gardens; and gardens just for strolling — all linked by meandering walkways, mulched paths, boulder steps, garden bridges, open meadows and rivulets flowing from two placid ponds. Landcape architect Armand Benedek's concept for this exceptional property, Twin Ponds in Westchester County, New York, offers outdoor rooms as such a logical extension of the indoors that their exploration and enjoyment is an invitation impossible to refuse.

The client, deeply interested in every aspect of his home's development, hoped to achieve not only the integration of Milton Klein's architecture and its surrounding landscape, but also to create new places for outdoor living. The house itself — interlocked concrete boxes bridged over an existing stream, cantilevered above a broad waterfall emanating from a courtyard swimming pool and fenestrated to provide broad views — provided the ideal base.

Equally ideal for Benedek's ecologically sensitive though highly varied design was the property's dramatic topography, with rock outcrops, open fields, woodlands and a circuitous watercourse that flows from a natural stream bed. As diverse as the adventures here may be, every addition seems appropriate for this site to accommodate. From formal to tree-canopied spaces, from secluded gardens to ever-changing pathways over bridges and down inclines to dense woodlands and sculpted hillocks, all form an inseparable blend.

A bridge spans a pond encompassed by weeping birch, yellow flag iris and hardy waterlilies [above]. *Various water plants and native shrubbery — including iris, waterlilies, azaleas and grasses — surround a waterfall* [opposite above]. *View of the house framed by a weeping katsura tree* [opposite below left] *and honey locust* [opposite below right].

Photography by Thomas K. Wanstall

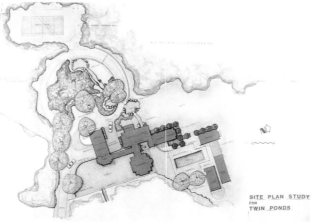

SITE PLAN STUDY
FOR
TWIN PONDS

A bonsai greenhouse bordered by hostas is set within a lush sweep of weeping Japanese maples, yellow flag iris and a stand of beech trees [opposite]. *A stone fisherman marks the crossover at the slab stone bridge* [left]. *At the lower pond, a bridge in a zigzag shape suggests a slow-paced walk through dwarf mugho pine, weeping Japanese maple and yellow flag iris* [below].

Mary Palmer Dargan, *Landscape Architect*
Jacksonville, Florida

Blending Two Traditions

The client bought the house next-door to her ancestral Cape Cod-style home in Jacksonville, Florida, as a convenient guest house for her children and grandchildren. Architecturally, it was 180 degrees opposite from the primary residence. Yet its Colonial Revival facade and low roofline, nestled into centuries-old live oaks, made it a prize worthy of the sensitive historic landscape preservation for which Mary Palmer Dargan is known.

In merging the two driveways into one, a weather-vaned garage separating the two houses became a clever carriage house. In addition, a skillfully designed loggia was needed to unite the two houses via an existing sunroom in one house and dining room in the other. When the client asked Dargan to suggest an appropriate architect, she volunteered Norman Askins of Atlanta, and the result has a gentle quality that avoids the look of a new addition.

"Making the Colonial's formal front suitable for a charming guest house subordinate to the original Cape Cod was a challenge," says Dargan. Her answer — an antique wishing well. Now axially related to the carriage house and new garden shed, and announcing the Colonial's front door, the wishing well brings an air of fantasy Dargan feels is so required of a guest house.

To unite the water frontage between the two homes, she shoehorned a rose garden with circular English steps into the newly acquired backyard of the Colonial Revival and the bulkhead that was extended to elevate the usable land. Including an astrolabe and hemispheric bench as well as roses and hydrangeas with which the client likes to decorate, this garden is a final note in Dargan's blend of languid, deep South plantings and English sophistication.

The colors of the rose garden perched on the edge of the St. John's River were chosen by the owner to accent the interior design of the two houses [above]. Curved bluestone English steps, custom-cut with rough edges to lend a feeling of age, provide a graceful transition to the rose garden from the guest house. Box shrub defines the garden, while lantana, plumbago and delphiniums cascade over the terrace [opposite].

Photography by Mary Palmer Dargan

The centerpiece of the rose
garden and informal
hydrangea garden is an astrolabe, made by Crowthers of
Syon Lodge, England, and set
on a hand-carved, cast-stone
base from Kenneth Lynch,
Connecticut. The curved,
unpainted teak bench is from
Weatherend [right]. The rose
beds are bordered with handmade Old Carolina brick from
Salisbury, North Carolina,
and set without mortar.
Sandshell paths are edged
with box shrub and pansies.
Delphiniums paired with boxwood anchor the terrace and
circular English steps [opposite
above]. The view from the
guest house encompasses the
garden building and antique
wishing well axially aligned
with the front door and its
entry of bluestone in a random ashlar pattern. Pairs of
box shrubs accent the bluestone around the wishing
well, which was purchased
from the Jack Warner estate
in Bel Air, California, and
was used in several movies
from the golden age of film
[opposite below].

Classic Accord

The climate is balmy in the Bahamas, and dispositions are too. At least they would all appear to be so if exemplified by the harmonious carrying-forth of this garden designed by architect Henry Melich.

Very much an extension of the formal, classical style of the single-story house that its owner, a widow, enjoys as a vacation retreat, the landscaping is in the Italian and French manner in which high hedges are often used to create outdoor rooms. Striving to achieve a dramatic effect that changes little over the seasons, Melich selected locally available plants wherever possible, including varieties of palms, broad hedges of multicolored bougainvillea and, on the southern side of the house, an abundance of plumbago, whose sky blue color happens to be the owner's favorite.

In and around the pond of the sunken garden, palms, crotons, bird-of-paradise, bromeliads, philodendrons and African iris are used to create a jungle effect.

The most fortuitous aspect occurred, however, when it was decided as an afterthought to create an 84-foot-long reflecting pool centered on the library to give full importance to the eighteenth-century statue, *Peace*, which the client and Melich discovered in London. The statue is one of a pair that stood at the entrance to Newgate Prison in London. It now looks perfectly at home and serene in its new surroundings.

An unforeseen use of the pool by the owner's grandchildren has been another plus of the design.

Placed between a formal row of Alexandria palms is one of a pair of stone jardinieres planted with multicolored portulaca. Yellow mandevilla vine grows up the wall from a base of hibiscus [above]. *Plumbago and yellow mandevilla vine present a colorfully abundant display on the side of the house that faces the golf course. The grass is St. Augustine* [right].

Photography by Roland Rose

*The library looks through a bower of yellow mandevilla
vine toward the reflecting pool that terminates at an
eighteenth-century statue,* Peace, *set against a backdrop of purple bougainvillea. Along both sides of the
pool are foxtail palms backed by a hedge of* Ficus
benjamina [above]. *A Jamaican palm towers over the
pool cabana and a ficus topiary tree* [opposite above].
An archway through an eleven-foot Ficus benjamina
*hedge leads from the pool to the garden. The statue is a
seventeenth-century heraldic lion* [opposite below].

Country Style

Elizabeth A. Lear, *Landscape Designer*
Long Island, New York

Country Villa Dressing

Situated in fields once cultivated with crops, the garden designed by Elizabeth A. Lear for Stone House on Long Island reflects not only the client's needs and tastes, but also the home's architectural vernacular and its recent past as a farm.

Stone House is the restoration and reinterpretation of a potato barn, probably built in the 1940s and graded and bermed for storage of potato crops. The landscape design addresses the renovation and change in identity, when the property became residential. Due to the character of the materials and existing elements, the structure's overall feeling is of a European country villa, with a rugged stone exterior complemented by softly-hued brick.

It was left to Lear's landscape design to satisfy the client's passion for classic historic garden form and flowers. "A successful floral designer with a large family, he requested a garden that would be monumental and romantic as well as usable for a wide variety of family activities," says Lear. "So we addressed these needs by first organizing the frame and structure of the terracing, courtyard and gardens, and lastly through the detailing."

The hardscape echoes the architecture's Pennsylvania-quarried stone and Danish-blend brick. Garden structures include a gazebo, arbor and pool house, all linked through the hardscape and plantings — arbor plants, parterre gardens edged in boxwood, large thuja hedging, specimen conifers and ornamental grasses.

Woven together in a sensitive plan offering enclosure and function yet retaining the site's feeling of openness and sky, the new design recognizes all architectural elements while expressing all clues therein regarding this land's native and cultivated vitality.

The front entrance courtyard, drive and retaining walls, graced with Japanese dogwood, arborvitae and weeping willow, are crafted in brick and stone, reflecting the architectural details of the house. The vertical planting structure further enforces this circular space, its shape repeated in the backyard gardens [above]. *The entry arbor frames a path, edged with small-leaved boxwood and dwarf English boxwood, leading through white birch trees to the inner courtyard terrace* [opposite].

Photography by Erika R. Shank

The terraces, softened by 'Eden' roses, provide hospitable living spaces that link home to landscape. The columned upper loggia, festooned with hanging beds of 'Alchymist' roses and 'Hyperion' daylilies, offers a view of the entire landscape [above].

The cutting/vegetable garden, the horticultural heart of Stone House where the owners delight in experimental annuals and edibles, is marked by little pickets and brick paths — informal, pastoral highlights of life in the country [top].   The columned wisteria arbor, made doubly abundant by a profusion of arborvitae and on axis with the dining room window, is an incision through the steep grades of the upper house and terraces and links them to the lower pool room and tennis court [above].

A Delicate Balance

Martha Stewart's early twentieth-century, shingle-style vacation residence is an excellent representative of the summer lifestyle of its time. When landscape architect Thomas Balsley first visited the property, it reflected a focus on summer breezes and beaches rather than labor-intensive gardening. In dramatic contrast, Stewart's primary interest was in entertaining within a landscaped garden environment.

The site design required a fresh look at the site/structure relationship, with Balsley relocating and condensing all driveway, drop-off, and parking functions, thereby preserving a significant area for formal gardens. The front yard is now a circular entertainment lawn framed by formal rose gardens — Martha Stewart's passion — and the formality continues around the house with a series of garden "rooms" and "doorways." An easing of this formality occurs at the eastern end of the property and along a moss-covered path shaded by hostas and ferns.

Garden architectural elements are critical components to the strength of the plan, including rose-covered arches inspired by Stewart and Balsley's joint visit to Claude Monet's garden in Giverny, France.

The rare collection of climbing roses and all other specimens in this extensive and diverse planting palette were spearheaded by Stewart, creating a lush garden that provides her with hours of visual and spiritual enjoyment each day. This, combined with the garden now accommodating up to one hundred guests, is testimony to the design's delicate balance of site planning with aesthetics.

Wooden stairs rise in three different places to the wraparound porch, its columns covered with lattice that in turn is home to a variety of climbing roses. Catmint flanks the front walkway. Hardy dwarf boxwood edges the brick and bluestone paths [above and opposite left].

Photography by Thomas W. Balsley

Painted steel arches, seasonally covered with roses, frame the view toward the statuary focal point beyond. The steel trellis structure at each entrance to the formal lawn is covered with wisteria [above right]. Hardy dwarf boxwood defines the croquet lawn, set against a variety of rose shrubs. The rose treillage sculpture is one of four [right].

Primrose Estate

Formal and natural areas are harmoniously blended in six acres of strolling gardens surrounding Primrose, the country estate in Indiana belonging to Mrs. Glenna Gibbs. The mother of New York designer Jamie Gibbs, Mrs. Gibbs uses the estate as a gathering place for her extended family of sixteen.

First established in the 1820s and heavily supplemented in the 1920s when the current finely-detailed, Art Deco masonry main house was built, the garden had been unattended for fifteen years when the Gibbses acquired it, making its restoration a primary challenge. Today, however, the sweeping rear and front lawns are bordered with shrubs that have been meticulously underplanted. A vast variety of deciduous and evergreen trees, ornamental shrubs and fruit orchards cover the property's gentle slopes and hills. And a 1.5-acre formal perennial garden ensures lavish blooms from late January to late November. The backdrop of farm fields and native woodland as well as artesian wells, a 1.2-acre, fully-stocked watershed pond and the family's requirement for abundant terraces and sitting areas influenced the orientation of additional plantings.

"The gardens provide me with the opportunity to cultivate old-fashioned plantings along with experimenting with new hybrids," says Jamie Gibbs. "They also give me the chance to renew myself, so I can return to the concrete canyons of Manhattan refreshed."

A wrought-iron arbor opens to the north end of the perennial garden, where drifts of color are provided by candytuft, Chinese lanterns, hibiscus and chrysanthemums supplemented by daylilies and completely underplanted with spring bulbs. The area is further supplemented by cannas and spider flower for summer color [above]. *The oldest area in the perennial garden is enclosed by clematis growing on old farm fencing* [opposite].

Photography by Jamie Gibbs

A native dogwood oversees a host of flowering crabapples, lilacs and mock orange [far left]. The pond-side path in mid-spring, with the flowering crabapples dropping their white petals over the perennial borders, is flanked by mature stands of French lilac, mock orange, rose of Sharon and yew [left]. A 'Cherokee Chief' flowering dogwood embellishes the rear terrace set against a backdrop of mature deciduous and evergreen trees. The dogwood is underplanted with lily of the valley, anemone and cinnamon fern. The more distant trees are underplanted with flowering shrubs and drifts of ground covers such as English ivy and dwarf periwinkle that, in turn, are underplanted with spring bulbs [below].

Pamela Burton, *Landscape Architect*
Los Angeles area, California

Lakeside Retreat

A family with children requested a tranquil garden on the same Los Angeles-area lakeside property where W. C. Fields retreated from nearby Hollywood. After Fields's original house was relocated to a child care center, Pamela Burton saved two historic sections of the site from demolition: the secret step-path through wild undergrowth to the lake and a fish fountain at the dock.

"Preserving these two separate relics enhanced the historic qualities of the new garden and made it seem as if we had interfered less arbitrarily with the past," says Burton. The major parts of the garden are organized into a series of terraces. The new house, designed by Thane Roberts Architects, opens onto a grand lawn bordered by perennials. Along one side, a rose-covered pergola forms a gateway to the pool area and the walkway that leads to a lookout for viewing the lake.

Stone pathways step down in terraces to a lower garden at the lakeside, where another path invites strollers to a quiet seating area adjacent to the secret step-path. Overhead, specimen sycamores and redwood trees mingle with majestic existing sycamores. The landscape's cumulative effect creates for the new house a comfortably settled feeling, the impression of being every bit as historic as its rejuvenated site.

Rising from the lake to enclose the pool are terraces planted with Photinia fraseri, *'Rosenka' bougainvillea, pittosporum and two old-fashioned roses. The lowest terrace wall incorporates a fountain preserved from the original estate* [above]. *Columns framing the entry and porch are covered with wisteria and bower vine. Grass and irises are planted between the stone pavers* [opposite left]

Photography by Pamela Burton
and Sasha Tarnopolsky

The pergola overlooking the lake is entwined with 'Cecile Brunner' roses, its stone support forming a grotto planted with jasmine, Siberian irises and mosses. The Santa Maria stone is set without mortar to allow it to develop a patina of lichens, mosses and liverworts [above right]. The lakeside path winds past flowering myrtle trees, camellias and California peppers, jasmine, honeysuckle and California native irises, toward a large native sycamore tree [right].

Summer Cottage Spirit

Every aspect of this garden, restored and improved by landscape designer Elizabeth A. Lear, was intended to address the classic perfection of the shingle-style summer cottage it surrounds.

Built on Long Island in 1870, Maidstone Hall had become hidden by large trees and a hodgepodge of overgrown plants. As this glorious house embraces many social events — croquet tournaments, weddings and garden parties — the owner wanted to create a more open feeling on the street side, to resolve a confused entry sequence, and to attain more privacy in the rear garden. Throughout the garden he wanted to continue the same degree of sophisticated elegance as his house and its nineteenth-century furnishings expressed.

Lear immediately attended to the restoration of the long line of white picket fence that gives definition to the front yard, rerouted the drive and paved it with Danish-blend brick, and removed some of the large trees. Now, the sensuous, open drive to the porte-cochère promotes a jubilant sense of arrival.

The wraparound porch leads to the backyard's romantic pleasure garden, where a classic rectangular pool, terraces of varying elevations, relocated trees and hedge have established new form and privacy. Complemented by Lear's careful selection of antique French rambler roses on the arbors, mixed perennials, ornamental shrubs and specimen trees, the new design graciously honors the refined yet buoyant spirit of Maidstone Hall.

A yew hedge banded with an annual white border of impatiens frames the trellis structure in the service entry area. 'Jeanne Lajoie' roses cascade between the obelisks articulating the view of the garage cupola and canopy of catalpa and horse chestnut trees [above]. *In the backyard, old-fashioned 'Jeanne Lajoie' rambler roses encircle the arbor, framing the vista across a manicured lawn to the magnificent arborvitae hedge* [opposite left].

Photography by Erika R. Shank

One of many cast stone urns, teeming with roses and skirted with nierembergia, framing the pool garden [above right]. Framing the wraparound porch leading to the backyard is a mixed herbaceous border of allium, spider flower, astilbe, snapdragons and 'Silver Dust' artemisia and edging of nierembergia [right].

Emmet L. Wemple, Warren W. Heideman, Joyce S. Sung
Emmet L. Wemple & Associates, *Landscape Architects*
Los Angeles, California

A Garden Sequence

The late Emmet L. Wemple, revered landscape architect, did not like straight lines. "Don't reveal everything at once," he used to say. "It's important to always be expecting something beyond the bend." In this garden that Wemple created with Walter W. Heideman and Joyce S. Sung, located on a five-acre site and used constantly by a large, multigenerational family, there is something beyond every bend, and it is always magical.

The entry drive, its expansiveness made possible due to the large residence, as well as barn, playhouse, tennis court and pool house being situated well back on the property, leads through high masonry walls and over a graceful curve of exposed aggregate, each unit separated with grass strips. All major trees, including a number of California live oaks and the entry's jacaranda, were preserved; others, including crape myrtle and a wide variety of fruit trees that augmented the existing ones, were added to lend shade and provide separation between the smaller gardens. Making each a glorious destination are masses of bougainvillea, orchids, gardenias, roses, honeysuckle and bromeliads enhanced by borders of perennials.

The sequential gardens are connected by walkways and paths, and the varied experiences of the gardens are enhanced by garden structures, fountains and a koi pond. A special note, almost totally concealed among the embracing oaks, is a giant-sized outdoor chess set, its chessmen serving as ever-present guards beside the grandchildren's playhouse hideaway.

The home is revealed through masses of pampas grass and displays of shasta daisies and daylilies [above]. *A boxwood parterre, filled with impatiens, surrounds the pond planted with iris and water lilies* [opposite].

Photography by Jay Venezia

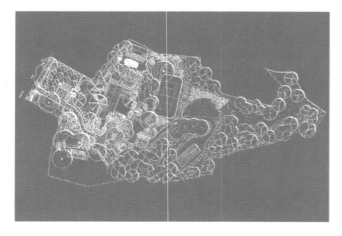

A grove of crape myrtle flanks the walk from the front door toward the driveway and is underplanted with white India hawthorn, escallonia and gardenias, as well as the property's ever-present masses of perennials — daylilies, calla lilies, dwarf agapanthus and fortnight lilies [above].

A king-size chessboard is composed of bricks of two different colors, complete with brick bench and porch to tie the game architecturally to the Morning Room/Playhouse [above]. A field of agapanthus weaves its way along a trellis, with citrus groves to the left [above right]. Various Victorian box trees lend their shade about a pool surrounded by shade-tolerant calla lilies, impatiens, ferns, heavenly bamboo and winter-blooming bergenia [right].

Joseph Minton, *Interior Designer*
Bruce Berger, *Landscape Architect*
Fort Worth, Texas

Verdant Seclusion

Decades ago, Fort Worth interior designer Joseph Minton developed the land around his 1930s Mediterranean-style cottage into a brick-walled haven graced with pool, fountain, fruit-bearing trees and abundantly planted terraces. Recently, however, he decided to remove the wall, which was visible from every window, and he spent so much time in his garden — entertaining family and friends or in tree-shaded contemplation — that he wanted more. So he purchased the property next door.

Summoning landscape architect Bruce Berger of Armstrong-Berger, he worked in close collaboration to extend his verdant seclusion to include a different view from every window, and expansive entertainment areas that would be strong visually as well as practical. The new area was also to receive Minton's pièce de résistance — a pergola in which stucco-covered concrete columns, entwined with wisteria and roses, rise over a stone floor to massive, protective cedar beams, while its rear wall is mirrored to double the garden's luxuriant viridity.

To complement the home's gray slate roof and its interior appointments of English and European antiques, Berger continued the country cottage garden feeling Minton had already established. Blue-and-white perennials, sumac, magnolia, dogwood and Japanese pine provide constantly changing visual delights along newly installed steppingstones and retaining walls. To lend further country-casual notes, he included wood fern, Boston ivy and native honeysuckle among the more formal specimens.

Says Minton, "A garden should express beauty and order — but also the wild, entrancing clutter of nature."

Agapanthus, yaupon trees and variegated elephant's ear leading to the home's gated entry set the richly textured tone that continues throughout the interior and the walled gardens beyond [above]. *Wooden doors that Joseph Minton acquired in Mexico conceal pool storage equipment, making an artful backdrop to this garden lush with elephant's ear, banana trees, regular and dwarf red bananas, pink hibiscus and espaliered elaeagnus* [opposite].

Photography by Ira Montgomery
Courtesy *Veranda*

The sunken garden was excavated two feet below what otherwise was flat property. The newly added steps of Oklahoma flagstone add architectural strength to the design [right].

Against a brick wall covered with Boston and English ivies, iron chairs and a daybed provide poolside comfort [left]. Clusters of potted, seasonal plants such as impatiens and sago palms give the garden additional variety and character [below left]. Views throughout the house only partially reveal the garden, serving as enticing invitations to walk outside [below]

Evergreen wisteria, trumpet creeper and
'Banksia' roses envelop the newly added
pergola, its aged appearance derived
from seventy-year-old beams salvaged
from a demolished commercial building
[opposite above]. *Retaining walls of
Arkansas flagstone are planted with
plumbago and agapanthus. Photinia
and sweet gum trees define a raised
seating area* [opposite below]. *The pergola
lends an intimate feeling to small gatherings, while the flat area planted in St.
Augustine grass can easily accommodate
up to fifteen tables* [left]

Directory

LANDSCAPE ARCHITECTS AND DESIGNERS

Thomas W. Balsley, ASLA
Thomas Balsley Associates
119 Fifth Avenue
New York, New York 10003
Tel: (212) 228-5588
Fax: (212) 228-5584

Armand Benedek, ASLA
Armand Benedek + Partners, Ltd.
Hunting Ridge Mall
Bedford, New York 10506
Tel: (914) 234-9666
Fax: (914) 234-6882

Bruce Berger, ASLA
Armstrong-Berger, Inc.
Landscape Architects and Planners
P.O. Box 191425
Dallas, Texas 75219
Tel: (214) 871-0893
Fax: (214) 871-0894

Gregory A. Boyer, ASLA
Greg Boyer-Hawaiian Landscapes, Inc.
47-410 Pulama Road
Kaneohe, Hawaii 96744
Tel: (808) 239-8264
Fax: (808) 239-7749

Pamela Burton, ASLA
Pamela Burton & Company
2324 Michigan Avenue
Santa Monica, California 90404
Tel: (310) 828-6373
Fax: (310) 828-8054

George Constant, ASID
425 East 63rd Street
New York, New York 10021
Tel: (212) 751-1907
Fax: (212) 832-0201

Christopher Cox, ASLA
Christopher Cox & Associates
969 Colorado Boulevard
Los Angeles, California 90041
Tel: (213) 257-0023
Fax: (213) 257-3036

Hugh Dargan, ASLA
Mary Palmer Dargan, ASLA
Hugh Dargan Associates, Inc.
515 East Paces Ferry Road
Atlanta, Georgia 30305
Tel: (404) 231-3889
Fax: (404) 848-9840

Zuhair H. Fayez
Zuhair Fayez and Associates
P.O. Box 5445
Jeddah
Saudi Arabia 21422
Tel: (966) 2 654 7171
Fax: (966) 2 654 3430

Randal Fujimoto, ASLA
1820 Algaroba Street, Suite 204
Honolulu, Hawaii 96826
Tel: (808) 942-5553
Fax: (808) 942-2228

Sidney Galper, ASLA
Cleo Baldon
Galper/Baldon Associates
723 Ocean Front Walk
Venice, California 90291
Tel: (310) 392-3992
Fax: (310) 392-9858

Jamie Gibbs
Jamie Gibbs and Associates
340 East 93rd Street
New York, New York 10128
Tel: (212) 722-7508
Fax: (212) 369-6332

Peter A. Gisolfi, AIA, ASLA
Iwona Rainer, RLA
Peter Gisolfi Associates
Landscape Architects, Architects
566 Warburton Avenue
Hastings-on-Hudson, New York 10706
Tel: (914) 478-3677
Fax: (914) 478-1600

Nancy Hammer
Nancy Hammer Landscape
Design, Inc.
81 Vine Street, Suite 302
Seattle, Washington 98121
Tel: (206) 441-1928
Fax: (206) 443-9277

Dennis Jenkins
Dennis Jenkins & Associates
5813 Southwest 68th Street
Miami, Florida 33143
Tel: (305) 665-6960
Fax: (305) 665-6971

Elizabeth A. Lear
Elizabeth Lear Landscape Associates
30 Main Street
Southampton, New York 11968
Tel: (516) 283-8649
Fax: (516) 287-4498

Ricardo Legorreta
Legorreta Arquitectos
Palacio de Versalles 285-A
Mexico City, Mexico 11020
Tel: (525) 251 96 98
Fax: (525) 596 61 62

Sunny McLean
Sunny McLean Showroom
3800 Northeast Second Avenue
Miami, Florida 33137
Tel: (305) 573-5943
Fax: (305) 573-1744

Stephen F. Mechler, ASLA
The Mechler Corporation
44-117 Kahinani Way
Kaneohe, Hawaii 96744
Tel: (808) 247-3109
Fax: (808) 247-3101

Henry Melich
Melich & White Architects
P.O. Box N3921
Nassau
Bahamas
Tel: (809) 327-8188
Fax: (809) 327-8863

Edward Micallef, MCSD, ASLA
FL 45 "Regent House"
Bisazza Str., Sliema SLM 15
Malta
Tel: (356) 319325/6
Fax: (356) 319324

Joseph Minton, ASID
Joseph Minton, Inc.
3320 West Seventh Street
Fort Worth, Texas 76107
Tel: (817) 332-3111
Fax: (817) 429-6111

Don Monger
The Landmark Group Pty Ltd.
Level 2 Oxley House
25 Donkin Street
South Brisbane, Queensland 4101
Australia
Tel: (61) 7 3846 7300
Fax: (61) 7 3846 7522

Shiro Nakane
Nakane Garden Research & Landscape
Consultant Corporation
1-6 Karatanouchi-cho
Taniguchi, Ukyo-ku,
Kyoto 616
Japan
Tel: (81) 75-465-2373
Fax: (81) 75-465-2374

Owen Peters, FASLA
EPT Landscape Architecture
1214 East Green Street
Pasadena, California 91106
Tel: (818) 795-2008
Fax: (818) 795-2547

Neiva Rizzotto
Rua Sofia, 75 Jardim Europa
01447-030 São Paulo, São Paulo
Brazil
Tel: (55) 11 852-1977
Fax: (55) 11 282-1385

**Peter Lindsay Schaudt, FAAR,
ASLA**
Peter Lindsay Schaudt Landscape
Architecture, Inc.
410 South Michigan Avenue, Suite 612
Chicago, Illinois 60605
Tel: (312) 922-9090
Fax: (312) 922-0536

Diane Sjoholm
Sirius - Fine Landscape Design
P.O. Box 1965
Sag Harbor, New York 11963
Tel: (516) 725-4091

Sherna Stewart
Sherna Stewart Design
Box 6145
Carmel, California 93921
Tel: (408) 624-8969
Fax: (408) 624-5126

Roger K. Warner
Roger Warner Garden Design
P.O. Box 331
St. Helena, California 94574
Tel: (707) 942-9372
Fax: (707) 942-8840

**Emmet L. Wemple,
FASLA** (deceased)
Denis L. Kurutz, ASLA
Frederick H. Haberecht, ASLA
Walter W. Heideman, ASLA
Joyce S. Sung, ASLA
Emmet L. Wemple & Associates
800 West First Street, #3003
Los Angeles, California 90012
Tel: (213) 382-9583
Fax: (213) 382-9184

John L. Wong, ASLA
The SWA Group
2200 Bridgeway Boulevard
Sausalito, California 94965
Tel: (415) 332-5100
Fax: (415) 332-0719

Mark Zeff
Mark Zeff Consulting Group, Inc.
260 West 72nd Street, Suite 12B
New York, New York 10023
Tel: (212) 580-7090
Fax: (212) 580-7181

PHOTOGRAPHERS

Thomas W. Balsley, ASLA
Thomas Balsley Associates
119 Fifth Avenue
New York, New York 10003
Tel: (212) 228-5588
Fax: (212) 228-5584

Pamela Burton, ASLA
Pamela Burton & Company
2324 Michigan Avenue
Santa Monica, California 90404
Tel: (310) 828-6373
Fax: (310) 828-8054

Mary Palmer Dargan, ASLA
Hugh Dargan Associates
515 East Paces Ferry Road
Atlanta, Georgia 30305
Tel: (404) 231-3889
Fax: (404) 848-9840

Tom Fox
The SWA Group
2200 Bridgeway Boulevard
Sausalito, California 94965
Tel: (415) 332-5100
Fax: (415) 332-0719

Don Freeman
Don Freeman Studio
3 Ninth Avenue
New York, New York 10014
Tel: (212) 989-2592

Jamie Gibbs
Jamie Gibbs and Associates
340 East 93rd Street
New York, New York 10128
Tel: (212) 722-7508
Fax: (212) 369-6332

Elizabeth Glasgow
P.O. Box 813
Sag Harbor, New York 11963
Tel: (516) 725-4745

Steven A. Gunther
Steven A. Gunther Photography
22050 Ybarra Road
Woodland Hills, California 91364
Tel: (818) 888-1029

David Knell
3 Banning Street
Wishart
Brisbane, Queensland 4122
Australia
Tel: (61) 7 3343 4461

Lourdes Legorreta
Sierra Nevada 460
Mexico City, Mexico 11000
Tel: (525) 520 07 45
Fax: (525) 520 40 45

Norman McGrath
Norman McGrath, Photographer
164 West 79th Street
New York, New York 10024
Tel: (212) 799-6422
Fax: (212) 799-1285

Edward Micallef, MCSD, ASLA
FL 45 "Regent House"
Bisazza Str., Sliema SLM 15
Malta
Tel: (356) 319325/6
Fax: (356) 319324

Ira Montgomery
Ira Montgomery Photography
2406 Converse
Dallas, Texas 75207
Tel: (214) 638-7288
Fax: (214) 638-7980

Shiro Nakane
Nakane Garden Research & Landscape
Consultant Corporation
1-6 Karatanouchi-cho
Taniguchi, Ukyo-ku,
Kyoto 616
Japan
Tel: (81) 75-465-2373
Fax: (81) 75-465-2374

Matthew Onyesco
1100 Carson Street
Seaside, California 93955
Tel: (408) 394-9808

Anthony Peres
645 Oxford Avenue
Venice, California 90291
Tel: (310) 821-1984

Gary D. Pietsch
Peach Boys Photo
22 Oneawa Street
Kailua, Hawaii 96734
Tel: (808) 261-4687

Lanny Provo
Lanny Provo Photography
100 Northeast 101st Street
Miami Shores, Florida 33138
Tel: (305) 756-0136

Roland Rose
Roland Rose Photographer
P.O. Box N9374
Nassau
Bahamas
Tel: (809) 327-8298

Augie Salbosa
Augie Salbosa Photography
1317 Kalukaua Avenue
Honolulu, Hawaii 96826
Tel: (808) 949-8598
Fax: (808) 955-6733

Leslie Schwartz
Leslie Schwartz Photography
2147 North Claremont
Chicago, Illinois 60647
Tel: (312) 276-3210

Erika R. Shank
Erika R. Shank Photography
Box 993
Amagansett, New York 11930
Tel: (516) 267-6735
Fax: (516) 267-6025

Mauricio Simonetti
Rua Francisco Cruz, 428-casa 4
São Paulo, São Paulo
Brazil
Tel: (55) 11 575 2917

Kipp Stewart
Box 6145
Carmel, California 93921
Tel: (408) 624-8969
Fax: (408) 624-5126

Eric Striffler
ESP
P.O. Box 215
Water Mill, New York 11976
Tel: (516) 726-7376
Fax: (516) 726-5972

Sasha Tarnopolsky
Pamela Burton & Company
2324 Michigan Avenue
Santa Monica, California 90404
Tel: (310) 828-6373
Fax: (310) 828-8054

Brett Uprichard
2150 Makanani Drive
Honolulu, Hawaii 96826
Tel: (808) 847-7431

Jay Venezia
1373 Edgecliffe Drive
Los Angeles, California 90026
Tel: (213) 665-7382

Ricardo de Vicq de Cumptich
Rua Pedro Teixeira, 91
São Paulo, São Paulo
Brazil
Tel: (55) 11 530-5549
Fax: (55) 11 530-5282

Peter Vitale
P.O. Box 10126
Santa Fe, New Mexico 87504
Tel: (505) 988-2558

Deidra Walpole
Deidra Walpole Photography
1569 North Topanga Boulevard
Topanga, California 90290
Tel: (310) 455-1722

Thomas K. Wanstall
Thomas K. Wanstall Photography
61 Fredrick Street
Yonkers, New York 10703
Tel: (914) 969-2531

Steven J. Young
Young Productions
431 North 34th Street, Suite B
Seattle, Washington 98103
Tel: (206) 634-0858

Zuhair Fayez and Associates
P.O. Box 5445
Jeddah
Saudi Arabia 21422
Tel: (966) 2 654 7171
Fax: (966) 2 654 3430

Index

Acknowledgments

Writing about gardens is not a simple task. For me it has been absolutely dependent on the many landscape design professionals who not only have shared in these pages some of the fine gardens that they have designed, but also their deep understanding of the environment. We have had long discussions about ecology, soil, climate, plant life and horticulture. I have learned from them something of the relationship between architecture, engineering, construction, irrigation and landscape history that influences their work on a daily basis.

Therefore, I would like to thank everyone whose designs appear in this volume. In particular, I would like to express appreciation to Christopher Cox, ASLA, Christopher Cox & Associates, and Thomas Balsley, ASLA, and Ron Hester, of Thomas Balsley Associates. They have gone out of their way to help me contact the appropriate people and include exemplary gardens in the pages of *Gardenscapes*.

To Jim Bauml, Ph.D., senior biologist at the Arboretum of Los Angeles County, I extend my deep appreciation. For he knew not who was calling him — almost everyday for months on end — yet helped me every time as I endeavored to sort out plant names, genus and species. When I could not reach Jim Bauml, Joan DeFato, the Arboretum's Plant Science librarian, would always come to my rescue. Much gratitude!

I am deeply indebted to the staff of PBC International for developing our presentation with the taste and precision that the subject and its practitioners deserve.

And once again I am overwhelmed by my great good fortune in knowing Angeline Vogl, my longtime associate since our days at *Designers West* magazine, and in her willingness to oversee every word in this manuscript.

A most special thank you to Martha Stewart not only for sharing her own garden designed with landscape architect Thomas Balsley in this volume but also for writing its welcoming foreword.

Finally, but really first of all, I would like to thank my husband Richard King for putting up with all my book writing in the midst of his own garden at our Arroyo del Rey.